INTRODUCTION

BRIGHT LIGHTS, BIG CITY

ARCHITECTURE AND THE ARTS

SPORTS AND RECREATION

NEIGHBOURHOODS

OUTSIDE TORONTO

This edition published by
Whitecap Books, Ltd.
1086 West Third Street
North Vancouver, B.C.
Canada V7P 3J6

Produced by
Bison Books Ltd.
Kimbolton House
117A Fulham Rd.
London SW3 6RL

ISBN 0-921061-84-6

Printed in Hong Kong

TORONTO

TEXT	JOSEPH ROMAIN AND JAMES DUPLACEY
DESIGN	JEAN MARTIN AND BEN KAHN

Whitecap Books
NORTH VANCOUVER, B.C., CANADA

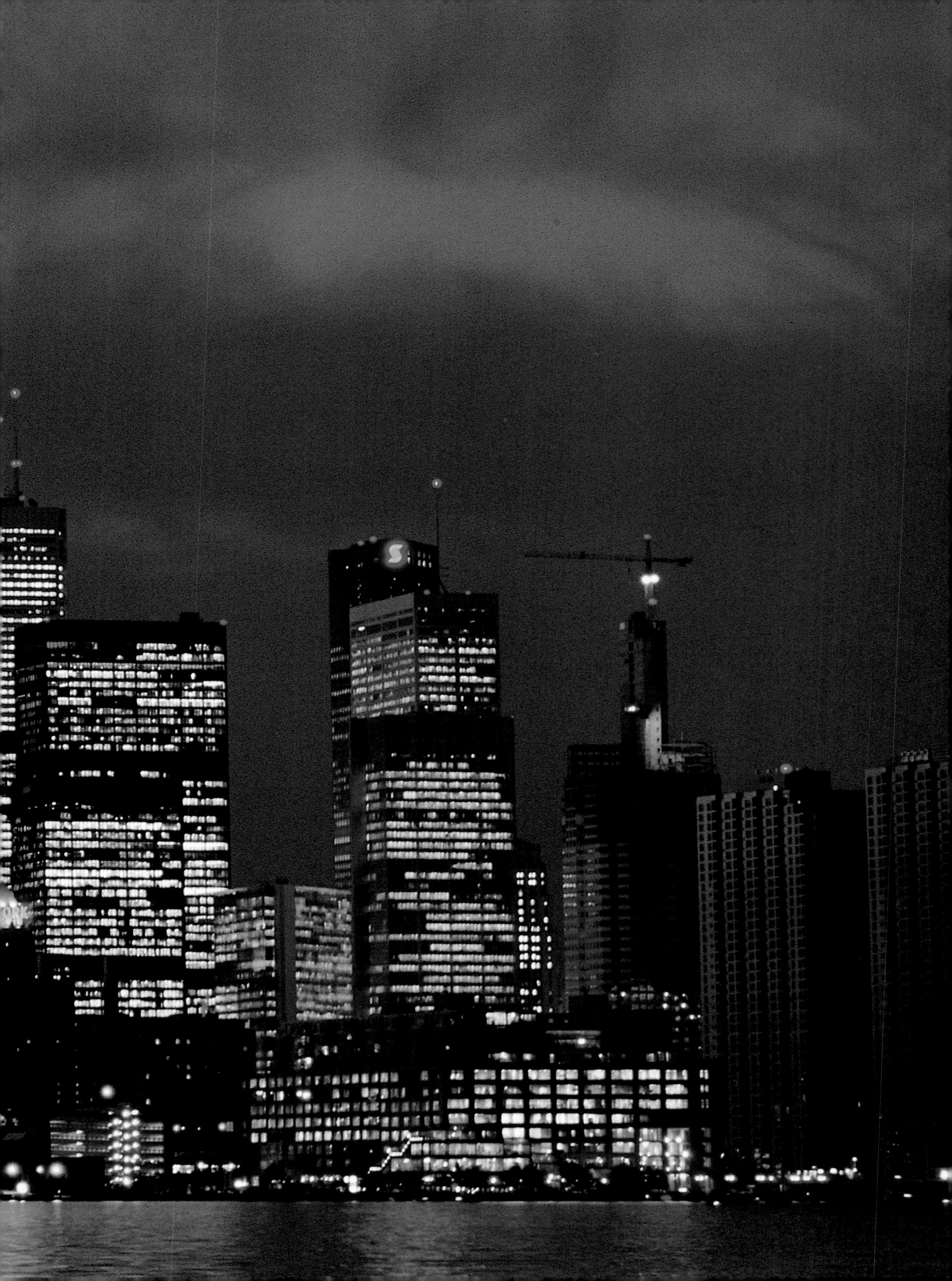

*3/6 The SkyDome, C.N. Tower and downtown
core of Toronto at night.*

INTRODUCTION

"Toronto will be a fine town when it's finished." Irish playwright Brendan Behan's comment is still relevant today. Toronto, Canada's largest city, continues to grow, and to flourish.

"Hog Town," as Ontario's capital city has been known, has a reputation for order, good government, and painstaking planning. The weeds are pulled, the shrubs are clipped, and the streets are clean. Students of city planning and residents alike have called Toronto "the city that works," "Toronto the Good" and "one of the most civilized places on earth." Visitors to Toronto remark on its well-ordered streets, its clean and efficient transit system, and the municipal pride of its residents. These factors are not the result of serendipity, but of the British colonial passion for order and organization.

A pausing place on a land route between Lake Huron and Lake Ontario, the Mississauga Indians called it *Toronto*, or "place of meeting." French fur traders used it as a storehouse as early as 1720. Following the American Revolution, British loyalists poured northward into the province of Upper Canada, and looked for a central place from which to govern the economy and political scene of the emerging colony. John Graves Simcoe, the first governor of Upper Canada, saw the "meeting place" as a logical point from which to monitor possible incursions from south of the border, and founded the town of York in 1793, named for Frederick, Duke of York. Simcoe was a tidy sort of man, and as early as the late 1700s had established a grid plan for the future town. Simcoe's desire was to bring to Upper Canada "a superior, more happy, and more polished form of government" in order to attract the Americans back into the British fold. The adjacent inland settlements made York a natural place from which to govern the fledging jurisdiction of Upper Canada.

The area surrounding the present city of Toronto is often referred to as the "golden horseshoe," because of economic overflow from the highly productive city. This was also true in the early days of the town of York. Fertile land and a fairly moderate climate gave settlers reasonable returns for their labours, and they would make the trek to the "meeting place" on Simcoe's roads, to the markets in "Muddy" York. The population of the town (approximately 700) was composed largely of British loyalists who had come north to escape republicanism; so when, during the War of 1812, the Americans twice pillaged the town, an anti-American sentiment developed, which has taken several generations to overcome.

A wave of British emigration brought farmers, merchants, skilled tradesmen and labourers to York, and by 1834, the population had swelled to 9000. That year, York was renamed Toronto. One of the leading forces in the city at the time was a printer, journalist, and general muckraker by the name of William Lyon Mackenzie. Mackenzie's liberal press, the *Colonial Advocate*, was the voice of revolution and dissent. Mackenzie became the first mayor in 1834, was defeated in 1836, and led the Upper Canadian Rebellion in 1837. This aborted storming of Yonge Street was intended to launch Upper Canada as an independent nation. Mackenzie, however, misjudged the tenor of the populace: He may have been a rabble rouser, but the population was not made up of rabble. Torontonians were, and are, a very conservative lot, for whom revolution is an idea worthy of debate, but not of action.

Many of the changes in the system of direct rule of the colony came about in due course, and the pride of independence, coupled with the security of belonging to a motherland, brought forth a burgeoning trade and manufacturing base. By the latter half of the nineteenth century, Toronto had established itself as the hub of English-speaking Canada. While Montreal still held the chair as Canada's most vital city, Toronto was busy establishing a large manufacturing and trading infrastructure, led by the family empires of the Masseys and the Eatons, and by the turn of the century the city was 150,000 strong. The makeup of the city was still largely British, but Europeans were increasingly making their homes in Toronto.

The economic base from which Toronto draws its wealth is incredibly varied, from textiles to foundries, from shipping to banking and from tourism to film-making. This diversified approach to development has served Toronto, Ontario, and Canada very well through depression and war. The city's ability to produce for the home market has been one of the important aspects of a development plan which is, unfortunately, under threat of change in the 1990s.

The city of Toronto has almost always been led by conservative politicians. When accused of being bland, one of Ontario's most successful politicians, William Davis, summed up the state of political life in Toronto and Ontario with the comment "Bland works." To say that the political leadership of Toronto is bland is not, however, to say that the political life of the city is boring. Each major development in the life of the city has been the topic of hot debate, public forums, and frequent acrimony. In the 1970s, reform mayors John Sewell and David Crombie institutionalized a climate of controlled development, thereby defending against laissez-faire construction in and around the municipality.

In the early 1950s it became economically advisable for cities in Canada to begin a process of amalgamation, and in 1953, Toronto joined with 13 neighbouring towns, boroughs and cities to form the Municipality of Metropolitan Toronto. Major public utilities were coordinated under this new level of government, giving Toronto a major influence in the federal system. Toronto does not often bring forth prime ministers, but unwise would be the government which excluded Toronto politicians from the cabinet table: The population of Metro Toronto includes more than 10 percent of all Canadian voters.

Since the late 1800s, public transportation has been a major component of life in Toronto. Thanks once again to Governor Simcoe's original grid plan, the city was arranged with a geometry very suitable to the installation of street car trollies. As the city developed eastward, westward and northward, the trollies rumbled further and further afield, bringing more and more people in and out of the core. The public transportation system, so popular throughout the decades, finally began to show signs of irretrievable over-use, and in 1949, construction began on an underground rail system. The subway, completed in 1954, was linked to other major arteries in the city's transportation system. Commuters are able to use formidable highways such as the 401, which runs between Montreal and Windsor, to arrive at the northernmost reaches of the city, and several major routes run from there into the centre of activity. The eastern Don Valley Parkway, bordered by a wide band of unspoiled greenery, brings automobile traffic to and from the centre of town. The Don Valley is linked to the Queen Elizabeth Way on the west of the city via the Gardiner Expressway, which parallels the waterfront and completes a circle of rapid highway transportation through and around the city.

Toronto, like most cities, is built on a major water transportation route. Lake Ontario is a central and pivotal body of water in the northern North American distribution route, and is a major part of the St. Lawrence Seaway system. Unlike many cities, however, Toronto has maintained a visual sense of being a city built on the water. Shipping and industrial use of Lake Ontario have left their scars on the waterfront, but the last 20 years have seen a valiant and largely successful effort to reclaim the land for public leisure and residential activities. The shore is dotted with waterfront parks, beaches, and marinas for the countless leisure craft, and residential developments abound on the waterfront at the centre of town.

Toronto is an attractive place to live. The many neighbourhoods, with their varying ethnic flavours, lend a cosmopolitan flavour to this originally British settlement. Restaurants of every description abound, the theatre scene is one of the world's most prolific, the business climate is very stable, and the social structure resembles that of cities in northern Europe. The educational environment allows for nearly every philosophy: Students have a wide choice of public, alternative, and private schools, and high schools are among the best available, tending to be institutions of learning rather than the battlefields and chaotic labyrinths found in other jurisdictions. Higher education opportunities range from the University of Toronto, a well-established and prestigious institution on three campuses, to the newer York University in the north of the city. Colleges range from the specialized Ontario College of Art and the Canadian Institute for Advanced Film Studies, through Ryerson Polytechnical Institute and the more general Sheridan, Centennial, Seneca, George Brown and Humber community colleges.

Toronto has more than its fair share of green spaces. Parks range in size and use from the large and beautiful downtown High Park, where urban dwellers flock on a weekend for walks, picnics, or cross-country skiing, to the "parkettes" often found adjacent to busy intersections which serve as pleasant breathing spaces. One could walk for days through the trails of the Don Valley and its connected series of nature preserves, and the waterfront, from east to west, is almost entirely negotiable by foot or bicycle.

The city is, by world standards, a safe place to walk, day or night. Because the downtown core has been well-maintained and is still a desirable residential location, people can mill about Yonge Street at all hours of the day without incident.

Toronto is a casebook for city planners. Development has been slower than some would like: Clearance to erect a building here or there requires painstaking explanations to city planners, exposure of corporate backers to the press and public, sometimes rowdy public meetings and media debates, and plenty of time. The frustration felt by developers is understandable, but the process of careful growth works well. Where many cities wrestle with the results of helter skelter development, Toronto looks forward to further planned development. From the founding of York in 1793 with a population of 700, to the current metropolis of some 2,300,000, Toronto has trimmed its shrubbery, cleaned its streets, and passed all manner of "obstructive" laws to maintain the orderly town envisioned by Governor Simcoe.

BRIGHT LIGHTS, BIG CITY

They call it "Toronto the Good," but don't tell them that on Yonge Street on a Saturday night. The business capital of Canada sheds its pinstripes after dark, and looks for a good time.

Many North American cities have seen their downtown cores deteriorate, and become unwelcome streets after dark. Not so in Toronto, where the heart of the city is still found in its main streets. The Yonge Street strip offers every kind of evening entertainment, from the quiet nuance of jazz at Sneaky Dee's Uptown to the clamour of heavy metal at Gasworks, and from the off-the-wall humour at Yuk Yuk's to the *Phantom of the Opera* at the Pantages Theatre. Browse in the record stores of Yonge and Dundas, stop and listen to the many street buskers, poets and clowns, or stop for a pint of the finest at the pub of your choice.

Just off Yonge Street is the "artist colony" of the Queen Street West Village. Every type of music, food and dress which fits the bohemian motif is in plentiful supply here on the "hard edge." Music? Any Canadian band who's going to make it, is going to make it here first. The Horseshoe Tavern is renowned for having broken the barriers between country and rock. The Rivoli offers a wide swath of performance art, New Wave music, poetry and good company, whereas Cameron House is the favourite haunt of those who like less structure in their music and more life in their conversation.

Toronto is the venue for one of the world's most respected cinema festivals. The Festival of Festivals, held in September of each year, features hundreds of films and the stars who create them. But the annual festival is only part of the scene: Numerous revue theatres, which offer seldom-seen gems on a regular basis, specialty movie houses, foreign language cinemas, and plentiful first-run theatres, combine to form an all-encompassing theatre community which is second to none.

Toronto does not restrict its dramatic life to the screen, for the stage community is among the most prolific in the world. The Canadian Stage Company, Tarragon Theatre, and Factory Theatre Lab are a few of the dozens of year-round production houses based in Toronto. Toronto's theatre community may be financially dominated by the blockbuster shows of the larger houses, but new Canadian plays can be seen regularly on the professional stages in and around the city. A short drive out of town brings one to Stratford, world-famous for classic enactments of the world's great English-language plays, or to the Shaw Festival, where the work of George Bernard Shaw is the bill of fare.

On the lighter side, Canada's Wonderland, Ontario Place and the Canadian National Exhibition feature the best of the world of amusement parks, with roller coasters, water rides, cotton candy and regular visits by big-name entertainers.

15 The burgeoning hub of Toronto's ever-growing downtown business district. The Scotiabank Tower with its distinctive red logo is the newest member of the high rise club, and a modern variant of the "flatiron" style.

16/17 A myriad of lights: a view of downtown and beyond from the C.N. Tower at night.

18/19 The Toronto banking community rules the skies above the Bay-King corridor.

20 The Ontario Hydro Building was designed to reflect the dominance of the resource industry in Canada. The building also reflects the people, streetcars, and buildings which depend on hydroelectric power as a major source of energy. Architect: Kenneth Cooper, 1975.

21 Day and night, the corner of Yonge and Bloor serves as the central crossroad in the life of the city.

22 The "Red Rockets" have served Toronto since
1861. Nearly 200 streetcars rumble back and
forth across the city 24 hours a day, 365 days a
year across 150 miles of track.

23 Sam The Record Man, Canada's largest and most popular record chain. The flagship store is located in the heart of Yonge Street, and is surrounded by large and highly competitive pretenders to its throne.

24/25 The new SkyDome looms above the elevated Gardiner Expressway, which forges a southern route east and west through the core of the city.

26 *A quiet scene in City Hall's Nathan Phillips Square, often the scene of celebration, demonstration, and exhibition.*

27 *Toronto's Metro Convention Centre, opened in 1987, is never quiet. Housing a hotel, theatres, exhibition areas and restaurants, and located at the foot of the C.N. Tower, it is one of the world's most desirable locations for business and pleasure.*

28 The garish Honest Ed's occupies an entire city block at the corner of Bloor and Bathurst streets. It may not be "haute couture," but it certainly is one of the most frequented stores in Canada.

29 Christmas at "The Ex." The Canadian National Exhibition is a late summer event, but the grounds are well-manicured year round.

30 The Toronto Symphony Orchestra in Roy Thomson Hall. The T.S.O. has been in business since 1922, and is currently under the musical direction of Gunther Herbig.

31 After years of success on the Broadway and London stages, the musical *Les Miserables* made a triumphant Canadian debut in Toronto during the summer of 1989. Housing the show is one of Toronto's most prestigious venues, the Royal Alexandra Theatre, better known simply as the Royal Alex.

32 The Ontario Science Centre, a provincial government agency, was built in 1969 by architect Raymond Moriyama. The Centre enjoys over one million visitors per year, and employs over 300 people to run the operation.

33 The Art Gallery of Ontario houses an impressive collection of 1400 pieces from Canada and around the world. The Henry Moore Sculpture Centre showcases a large exhibition of his unique and massive human forms. The exhibition changes periodically, with selections from the hundreds of pieces which represent the world's largest public collection of his work.

34/35 Ontario Place, just south of the C.N.E. grounds, is an architectural marvel which encompasses Canada's first IMAX theatre (inside the geodesic dome), a wide variety of restaurants, a large marina, an amusement park, Canada's Baseball Hall of Fame and the Ontario Place Forum, where top-name entertainers thrill hundreds of thousands each summer.

36/37 With the Canadian National Exhibition in full swing, the cityscape is upstaged by the bright lights of the midway.

ARCHITECTURE AND THE ARTS

By world standards, Toronto has a short, yet rich architectural history. As is the case in many North American cities, Toronto has recycled designs from around the globe, and has evolved into a showcase of architectural styles.

For many admirers of architectural history, places of worship are a central point of interest. Toronto offers a wealth of beautiful examples, from the Gothic Revival of Timothy Eaton Church and the Church of the Holy Trinity, to the Romanesque Revival of the Holy Blossom Synagogue. Ste. Anne's Church on Gladstone Avenue, designed by Ford Howland in 1907, offers a wonderful example of Byzantine Revival.

Bankers also grace the city streets with elaborate constructions which stand as monuments to their powerful trade. The most important bank in Canada during the nineteenth century was the Bank of Montreal. This institution's most elaborate construction can be found at the corner of Front and Yonge streets, and is a rare and beautiful example of the High Victorian style used during the late nineteenth century. From the Art Deco flavour of the Bank of Nova Scotia on King Street West, to the Beaux Arts design of the Dominion Bank building at King and Yonge, it is clear that the financial community has made a significant impact on the architectural life of the city in the last century. The bankers did not leave off in the last century, however: Toronto's skyline is dominated by the concrete and glass of Commerce Court, the new Scotiabank Tower, and the glittering Royal Bank Plaza. The latter is comprised of two golden towers, whose reflective glass shimmers with the 2500 ounces of gold which went into the glass manufacturing process.

Another strong force in the development of architectural history in Toronto has been the men and women who have governed the city. The most striking of the government buildings is Toronto City Hall, designed and completed in 1965 by Viljo Revell. The two semicircular towers encase a saucer-shaped council chamber, which itself is perched atop a podium structure. Housing all the expected services, including two public libraries, Revell's design succeeded in creating a focus for public activity: Nathan Phillips Square, to the immediate south of the structure, hosts events of every description, from ice skating to the circus.

The Ontario Legislature building, located at Queen's Park Circle, is a much older, though no less interesting, example of public architecture. This structure, built in 1886 by R.A. Waite, is the last of four such buildings created for the purpose of governing the province. The broad main entrance is comprised of three wide arches which are echoed by corresponding arched windows in the chamber above. Guided tours of the building cover the intricate and somber detail of the interior panelling, the reconstructed west wing, and a breath-taking high-relief carving of the Ontario coat of arms.

Elaborate residential architecture can best be seen in Toronto's Rosedale, Fallingbrook, Forest Hill, and High Park, where the desirability of the neighbourhood and the powerful real estate market has ensured the maintenance of these homes of the rich and famous. Not to be overlooked are the former mansions which have been put to other purposes: The Massey House and The Cooper House, both in the Sherbourne-Jarvis district, are well worth visiting. Perhaps the single most elaborate example of residential architecture is Casa Loma, the dream home of Sir Henry Pellatt. This castle on the hill boasts three bowling alleys, 30 bathrooms, 25 fireplaces, a marble swimming pool, and a shooting gallery. Pellatt did not live long in Casa Loma, but his elaborate dream makes for a wonderful way to pass a rainy day of sight-seeing in Toronto.

39 The C.N. Tower, the world's largest free-standing structure (1815 feet) shares its pedestal of architectural majesty with the SkyDome, the world's first retractable roof stadium. Together they form an unbeatable team in the competition for the entertainment dollar.

40/41 A study in forms: the sharp lines of the buildings of the downtown core are etched severely behind the great curve of the SkyDome roof.

42 Michael Snow captures the flavour of the modern sporting experience in his sculpture appropriately named "The Fans." These cheering, jeering and leering characters welcome visitors to SkyDome.

43 This photo, taken from high above the city, shows off some of Toronto's most treasured structural features. Aside from the central attraction, the SkyDome fully retracted, the C.N. Tower, the Roy Thomson Hall, Union Station, Sheraton Centre, City Hall and the Royal York Hotel are also notable.

44/45 Sunset colours the skyscrapers of the downtown core.

46 In 1977, Zeidler-Roberts Ltd. completed the first phase of the Eaton Centre, at that time the largest and most lavish retail complex of its kind. Today three levels of retail stores provide the avid shopper with plenty to do on a rainy afternoon downtown.

47 When it was completed in 1965, Toronto's City Hall was a marvel of the modern artform. In 1958, a world-wide competition was held for the design, and by 1961, Viljo Revell's winning design began to take shape. Today it remains one of the most unique and respected works of architecture not only in Toronto, but also in the world.

48/49 A view of the curving towers of the City Hall.

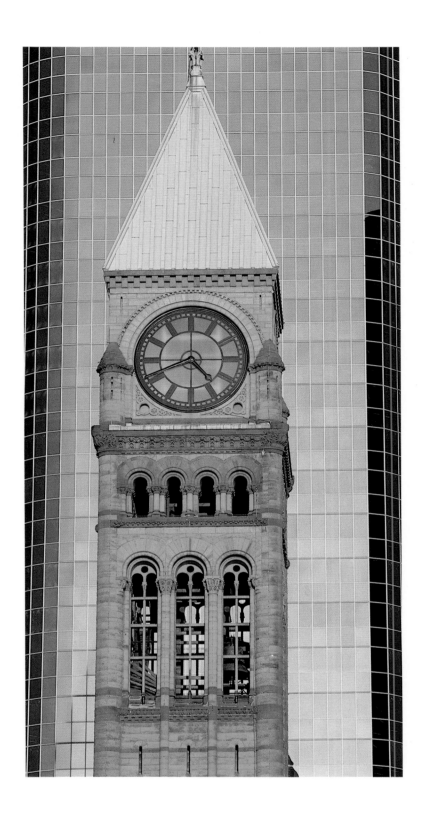

50 The old reflected in the new: Toronto's Old
City Hall, now functioning as a court building,
was built in 1899 by Toronto architect E.J.
Lennox.

51 The bell tower in Old City Hall. Built using
blocks of Credit Valley stone and New Brunswick
brownstone, the resulting finish is one of con-
trasting colour and texture.

52 Casa Loma was built in 1911 by Sir Henry Pellatt, a British aristocrat who had always wanted his own castle. Today it is under the authority of the Kiwanis Club of Toronto, and daily tours are conducted by interpreters in period costume.

53 Longtime Toronto residents remember the Royal York Hotel as the dominant feature on the skyline since 1929. Today, this aging matron is dwarfed in size by neighbouring twentieth-century monoliths, but few can match it for elegance, style, and old-world polish. Architects: Ross & McDonald.

54/55 Built in 1894 by the ubiquitous manufacturing family, the Masseys, Massey Hall is one of the most intimate, plush, and comfortable stages in Canada. The building was a gift to the city from Hart Massey, the farm machinery magnate. Architects: S.R. Badgley & G.M. Miller.

56/57 The Roy Thomson Hall replaced Massey Hall as the home of the Toronto Symphony Orchestra in 1982. Architect: Arthur Erikson.

58/59 The "pop-nautical" Ontario Place, opened in 1971, was designed by the firm of Craig, Zeidler, Strong.

60 Queen's Park is the seat of government for the province of Ontario. The building was completed in 1892, and by 1893 was bustling with the business of governing the province. Architect: Richard Waite.

61 Osgoode Hall and its "Cow's Gates." When Osgoode Hall was established in 1832, it was located on the outskirts of the city. One of the major problems with the site was the presence of pasturing cows in the neighbourhood, and as a result, an elaborate wrought iron fence with special gates was built to allow the law students in, and keep the bovines out. Today there is little chance of herds of cows invading the campus, located at the very busy intersection of Queen Street West and University Avenue.

08:48 VIA DEPARTURES DÉPARTS 08:48

↓	Arrivals		Arrivées
↓	Baggage Pick-up		Bagages entrants
↓	GO Trains		Trains GO
↓	Subway		Métro
↓	Royal York Hotel		Hôtel Royal York
←	Departure Gates 4-13		Portes départ 4-13

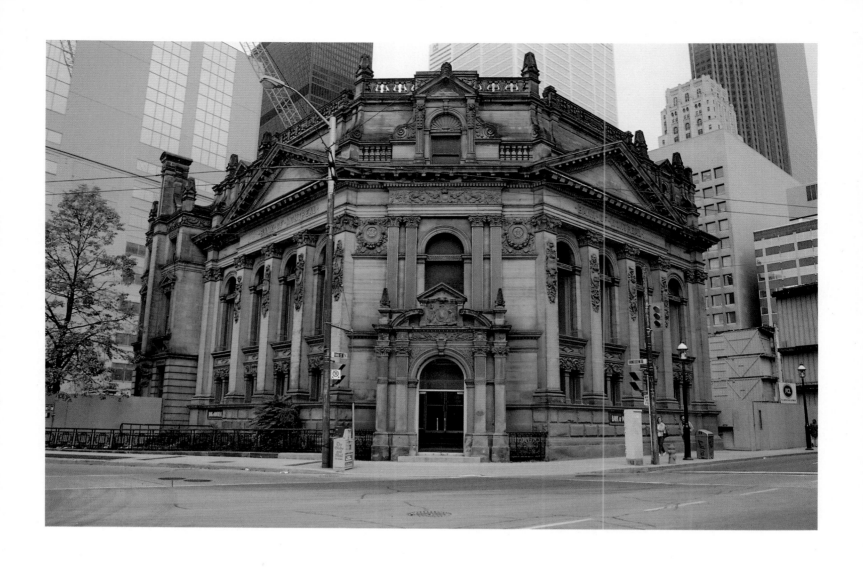

62 Virtually every passenger who crosses the country must pass through Union Station, the largest and most elaborate of its kind. For those interested in fine architectural detail, Union Station is an important place to visit. Architects: Lyle, Ross and McDonald, Jones, 1927.

63 The old Bank of Montreal building is the new headquarters of the Hockey Hall of Fame and Museum.

64 Architect David Roberts Jr. was challenged to design a building for a very irregular intersection. The result is the Gooderham "Flatiron" Building. On the other side of the building is an interesting mural by Derek Besant, added in 1980.

65 St. James Cathedral was built in 1853 by Cumberland and Rideout for Bishop John Strachan. The tower and spire, at 306 feet, are the tallest in Canada.

66 The two triangular office towers which make up the Royal Bank Plaza are encased in gold tinted reflective glass; 2500 ounces of gold were used to prepare the glass for this project. Architects: Webb, Qerafa, Menkes, Housden, 1977.

67 The University of Toronto is a myriad of architectural styles and neighbourhoods. About 53,000 students attend the University and its six associated colleges in its more than 300 buildings.

SPORTS AND RECREATION

Americans know Toronto as the home of the Blue Jays; Canadians revere it as the home of the Maple Leafs. But there is much more to the sporting community than these two highly-successful professional franchises. The Argos, the Canadian Football League's oldest franchise, have been playing ball since 1873, and boast a successful and proud record of longevity. Toronto is home to two professional soccer teams, the Blizzard and the North York Rockets, both members of the Canadian Soccer League.

The Toronto Maple Leafs have not been in evidence at the top of the NHL over the past few years, but they are still Number One in the hearts of many Canadian sports fans. Aside from Montreal, Toronto has won more Stanley Cups than has any other team. The Blue Jays, who came onto the American League scene in 1977, have been, arguably, the most successful expansion franchise in baseball history. Though they are yet to drink champagne at the World Series, they have captured two Eastern Division pennants, and in 1989 set an American League attendance record by drawing over 3.4 million fans to their new home, SkyDome.

If you like the ponies, Toronto is your kind of town. The annual Queens Plate is the most highly recognizable jewel in the Canadian Triple Crown, and is the oldest international stakes race on the continent. No two-bit horses here, as the world's finest in the racing community gather in their glad rags and lay down big money on this most prestigious of Canadian races.

The Molson Indy is an annual formula race held on the Exhibition Grounds in the heat of July. Though only in its fourth year of existence, it attracts the world's best drivers and the largest crowds for any sporting event in Canada.

Within a few minute's walk, a visitor can see the Hockey Hall of Fame and Museum, Canada's Sports Hall of Fame, and the Canadian Baseball Hall of Fame where the heritage of the nation's sporting life is there for all to see.

Toronto is a big sporting town, but other recreational delights abound. The zoo is among the best in the world, with 4000 animals of all sizes, shapes, and descriptions. A trip to the zoo is special in the winter, when the snow is deep: cross-country trails bring you around the world in much less than eighty days.

Toronto's museums entertain and educate. The Royal Ontario Museum is the largest in the city, boasting a world-renowned dinosaur exhibit, an intelligent look at the heritage of Canada's native peoples, an exhaustive natural history section, and frequent blockbuster touring shows.

Across the harbour is Toronto Island, where the pace is slower than on the mainland. Although they are the home of a small number of Torontonians, the islands are mostly parkland and marinas. A sunny day can be pleasantly spent wandering along the beach, through the narrow pathways, and at the children's zoo.

There's plenty to do in Toronto; the Ontario Science Centre challenges the imagination, Fort York offers a look at the early military history of the city, and Black Creek Pioneer Village provides a well-rehearsed study of pioneer life. The Metro Toronto Convention and Visitor Association provides information specialists to help the visitor find the best of what the city has to offer.

69 Sailing on Lake Ontario. The multitude of marinas in and around the Toronto city limits attests to the fact that sailing is a favoured sport among the upwardly mobile.

70 Ontario Place is, among other things, a water-based theme park. In a new twist on the bumper car, here we see the "bumper boat." Beyond is the HMCS Haida, a World War II Tribal Class destroyer. Canada's most famous warship, it is the last of the 28 of its kind built during the war. Moored at Ontario Place since 1971, it is a popular attraction for all seafaring enthusiasts.

71 The "Ned Hanlan," a tug which did service in Toronto Harbour from 1932 to 1966, was the last steam-powered tug in the business. Today, it sits in dry dock outside the Marine Museum of Upper Canada, which tells the story of the changing face of the Great Lakes marine traffic.

72 For over 110 years Canadians have made the trek to the Canadian National Exhibition. The C.N.E. attracts more than two million visitors annually.

73 Toronto is host to the world's largest offshore fireworks festival in the world. Pyrotechnists from around the world come to compete in this exhibition of fire over the water.

74/75 Canada's Wonderland, located just north of Toronto, features amusements for all ages, live big-name entertainment and some of the world's most elaborate roller coasters.

76/77 Toronto's waterfront is accessible, picturesque and the subject of much debate between conservationists and developers. Here at Humber Bay Park, the conservationists have clearly been the winners.

78/79 High Park, in Toronto's west end, offers peace and beauty in all four seasons.

80 The Metropolitan Toronto Zoo exhibits over 4000 animals on over 700 acres in an open-concept, geographically arranged park.

81 Centreville on Toronto Island is the perfect place to spend a summer day with children. Starting with a ferry ride across to the island, children can feed the birds, visit a small petting zoo, and enjoy inexpensive rides in the shady environs of the park. A short walk to the beach for a picnic, a ride on a rented pedal car, and back to the ferry docks makes for relaxed parents and very tired and happy children.

82/83 The Toronto Argonauts have been in competition for the Grey Cup since the Governor General, The Earl of Grey, donated it in 1909. In the ensuing 80 years of competition, the Argos have had their names engraved a record eleven times on the silver mug that is emblematic of the champions of the Canadian Football League.

84/85 SkyDome is the new home of the American League Baseball franchise the Toronto Blue Jays. The move into the facility on 5 June 1989 enabled the Jays to set an American League attendance record with more than 3.4 million fans rumbling through the turnstiles during the 1989 division-winning season.

86 George Bell of the Toronto Blue Jays. Since joining the American League's East Division in 1977, the Blue Jays have been a resounding success, both on the field and at the box-office. Now playing at their new home in SkyDome, the Jays are ready to showcase their team to the world in a facility deserving of their talents.

87 The Toronto Maple Leafs in action at Maple Leaf Gardens. Though the Leafs have been cellar rats in recent years, they have a proud tradition of shooting and scoring that goes back to the inception of the NHL.

88 (top) The tradition of the Redcoats lives on at Toronto's Fort York. Once a force to be reckoned with, today the fort demonstrates its proud past for tourists, students and history buffs.

88 (bottom) The Queens Park marching band continues a tradition from the days of yore.

89 At Black Creek Pioneer Village in the northwest of the city, visitors can see what life in pioneering days was like and meet interpreters who exhibit the daily routines known to early Ontario settlers.

NEIGHBOURHOODS

The waves of immigration through the twentieth century have brought Toronto an interesting pattern of settlement which is very different from that of the United States. The Canadian experience has been that as immigrant populations settle, they retain a strong sense of their cultural identity. Where the American model has been the melting pot, the Canadian counterpart has been the mosaic.

In Toronto, each wave of immigration has brought its problems for the immigrants, and adjustments for those already settled. When the Irish came to Toronto, they were not welcomed by the English and the Scots, who had settled the Indian lands. Signs hung outside of shops reading "Help Wanted: No Irish Need Apply." The Irish immigrants found themselves at the bottom of the social scale, and not particularly wanted in their new homes. As the Irish settled down in Cabbagetown, European immigration brought Jews, Italians and Ukrainians into the city's mosaic. Once again, they were welcomed in similar fashion, and found themselves in their own neighbourhoods, and on the bottom of the social strata. What became unique and interesting about this pattern of migration to Toronto is that each of these immigrant populations maintained its ethnic flavour, rather than becoming "Anglicized." The Italian population of Toronto still sees itself as Italian-Canadian, the Greeks as Greek-Canadians and so on. Not only is there a sense of unity, a geographical base, and an economic web which services each of the cultural groups, but one can hear it in the accents, see it in the home decor, and sense it in the markets.

On the west end of the city, in and around Roncesvalles Avenue, a large and evident Polish community has become ensconced. The many grocers and delicatessens boast home-made sausage, pierogies, cabbage preparations and some of the finest meats available in Toronto. The shopkeepers greet patrons in their native Polish, and stock newspapers from home and from Polish language presses in Toronto.

In the centre of the city, at Dundas and Ossington streets, the fish markets signal the community of Little Portugal. From the elaborate churches to the costumes, parades and ceremonies of the annual communion celebrations, this neighbourhood is alive with the flavour of Portugal.

Only blocks away, on the way to Chinatown, is the Kensington Market area, where many cultures meet in a feast of sights, sounds and smells of the world. Fishmongers display their wares on the narrow sidewalks, while from West Indian clothing emporiums, rhythms of the islands pour out onto the street. Italian baked goods, kosher meats, and cheeses from around the globe are a few of the items available at this cross-cultural centre.

Most Torontonians think of Chinatown as centred around Dundas Street and Spadina Avenue, but in fact it stretches in all directions and for many blocks. Chinese greens, herbs, medicines, clothing, reading materials, and of course, meals abound in this centre of the Asian community.

In the east end of the city, at Coxwell and Gerrard streets, is a community which is rapidly becoming "Little India." Clothing stores specialize in saris, restaurants serve up chutney, peas and curry, and the language of commerce was once heard only in the Orient.

The variety of the city's ethnic communities can perhaps best be sampled by a long walk or drive along the length of Bloor Street and its eastern ally, Danforth Avenue. From the rich flavours of Italian gelati to the shish kebab of Greektown, one will find a plethora of foods prepared, languages spoken, and religions practiced. Each neighourhood, with its own distinct heritage, proves to be a rich lesson in cultural history for the tourist and resident alike.

91 Queen Street runs the length of the city from east to west, but seems to pass through most of the known world. Each block turns up another world of ethnic costume, language and lifestyle.

92/93 The colourful homes of Lisgar Street, in the heart of the Portuguese district.

94/95 Dundas Street in Chinatown is brightly lit with neon at night.

96/97 Kensington Market, Canada's cultural crossroad, is the most famous world market in Canada.

98 A wide variety of faiths are represented in houses of worship in this cosmopolitan metropolis. Here, two men converse on the steps of the synagogue at Bathurst and Lawrence.

99 A statue of Pope John Paul II stands in the square in the Polish neighbourhood of Roncesvalles.

100/101 The Beaches. This old and close-knit community is one of the most pleasant and prestigious neighbourhoods in the city. Kew Beach Park boasts a long and lovely wooden boardwalk which meanders along the unspoiled sandy shoreline of Lake Ontario.

102/103 The hustle and bustle of the city is forgotten in the tranquil surroundings of Broadview Park. The park is built on the long and sloping bank of the Don Valley.

104 (top) Toronto is home to one of the largest Italian communities in the world.

104 (bottom) Independent merchants stock just about anything known to man in Kensington Market.

105 A Greek wedding on Pape and Danforth.

106 These steel drum makers provide a large West Indian community with musical instruments which ring with the rhythms of home.

107 The Caribana Festival parade brings an ancient tradition to the new world. Growing in strength with each passing year, the festival has become one of the highlights of the summer.

108/109 The Real Jerk restaurant on Broadview and Queen,which serves up West Indian fare, is one of many excellent ethnic restaurants in the city.

110 The hard edge of the Queen Street West Village, Toronto's haunt for hip fashion.

111 The Bamboo Club on Queen Street West rings with tropical sounds and attracts trendy people. P.I.B.s (persons in black) pervade the district, home of bookstores, art galleries, chic restaurants and post-modern fashions.

112 Nowhere in the developed world will you find more hospitable neighbourhoods than those of Toronto's island communities. Here on Ward's Island, the residents have their own community centre, school, and community association. Mostly peopled by the upwardly mobile, the inconvenience of the ferry "curfew" is outweighed by the close-knit feeling of island life.

113 *The Rosedale neighbourhood is home to wealthy downtown residents. The area offers all the convenience of the city with the ambience of the suburbs.*

OUTSIDE TORONTO

Toronto is located at the centre of what is called the "golden horseshoe." As the focus for economic activity for the Ontario region, Toronto has always spilled over into the surrounding environs. Former "bedroom communities" have in recent years taken on lives of their own in, among other places, Markham, Unionville, Thornhill, Richmond Hill, and Mississauga.

Further afield are such communities as Oakville and Oshawa, which have had a healthy industrial base for many years, but as the big city has grown, have found themselves growing more and more a part of it. Oakville is the home of the Glen Abbey Golf and Country Club, a world standard facility designed by Jack Nicklaus. Each year it hosts the Canadian Open Golf Championship. Oshawa is the location of the huge General Motors plant; if you've purchased a General Motors car in Canada, it's safe to say that it rolled off the line in Oshawa.

Today when we refer to Toronto, we often include places like Scarborough, North York, East York, and Etobicoke, though they are large enough to have their own neighbourhoods, character, and urban problems. The sense of controlled development has come late to these partners in the Metro Region, and the boom periods of the recent past have sprouted interesting urban configurations which are well worth a visit. Some of the most elaborate shopping malls can be found in these communities. The Scarborough Town Centre sprawls for what would be city blocks; and the Bayview Village Shopping Centre is the modern, suburban answer to a downtown strip.

While most of these centres fall into the descriptive mold of "suburbs," they each have a distinct personality and character. They are not content merely to be part of Metropolitan Toronto—they strive to create their own unique identities. Many have their own theatre communities and artists' groups, and some of the more successful amateur sport teams come from these areas. North York is a favoured location for a new multi-purpose sports and entertainment facility, which may become the new home of the Toronto Maple Leafs and possibly the home of a new National Basketball Association franchise. As Toronto spreads its wings and stretches further east, west and north, these districts will play an even greater role in the emergence of Toronto as a city of universal appeal.

115 From high atop the picturesque Scarborough Bluffs, one can see miles of coastline, cityscape, and undeveloped shores.

116 The name "Scarborough" might conjure up visions of pastoral countryside, but nothing could be further from the truth. This burgeoning city sprouts high-rise office towers and apartment complexes at a breathtaking rate.

117 To the west of Toronto is Mississauga, a rapidly expanding city which is developing a personality of its own. Formerly a "bedroom community," Mississauga today can hold its own against most emerging cities.

118 Rarely is a town centre named for an incumbent mayor. Mel Lastman, Mayor of North York and namesake of Mel Lastman Square, is so colourful and dedicated that the exception was well-received by the public.

119 Modern architecture and midday bustle in North York.

120/121 Thousands of cars surround the General Motors plant in Oshawa. GM is the major employer in Oshawa, located 30 miles east of Toronto.

122 GO Transit links Toronto with the many communities which surround it.

123 An aerial view of the railyards in North Toronto. Passenger rail in Canada is about to take a major shunt into oblivion. The fate of the freight train is still unknown, but its days, too, may soon be numbered.

124/125 The affluent community of Oakville is just a few minutes from the heart of the big city. Many commuters make the journey daily to and from this sleepy town of green trees and blue pools.

126/127 The late afternoon sun illuminates a line of willows in Mississauga.